D0540880

• DOCTORS •

FROM THE EARLY YEARS OF PUNCH

• DOCTORS •

The Lighter Side of Medicine

AT HOME

The successful Doctor

Special edition for Past Times

Robinson Publishing Ltd.
7, Kensington Church Court
London W8 4SP

This edition published by arrangement with Punch Ltd.
copyright © Punch Limited 1998

For 'Heal Thyself', copyright © Richard Gordon 1953
acknowledgement is made to Curtis Brown

*A CIP catalogue record of this book is available
from the British Library*

ISBN 1–84119–005–5

Design and computer page make up
Penny Mills
Printed and bound in the EC

PAST TIMES®

• CONTENTS •

'To be perfectly frank, my dear lady, no, I can't hear a "funny humming noise."'

· DOCTOR ·
AND
PATIENT

COLLEGE OF
GENERAL PRACTITIONERS
[1845]

A scheme, it appears, has been set on foot for the establishment of a 'College of General Practitioners.' Now, since diseases, very generally, are either imaginary, or such as would get well of themselves if let alone, one highly important branch of General Practice is the treatment of cases which do not require it. The General Practitioner, though not a Consulting Physician, must consult his own interest. *Verb. sat. sap.* but if the College Examiners are not saps, they may take a hint from *Punch.* Teachers must first be taught; and here, for the benefit of those whom it may concern, is a little APPROPRIATE EXAMINATION PAPER:

Appropriate Examination Paper:
with Answers.

Q. If you asked a patient to put out his tongue and found it perfectly clean, what would you do?

A. Shake my head, and say, 'Ah!' or 'Hum!'

Q. What is the meaning of 'Hum,' Sir?

A. It means: '*I* see what is the matter with you.'

Specialist: 'But, my dear Madam, I can find absolutely *nothing* wrong with you. Can't you —er *suggest* something?'

Appropriate Examination Paper:
with Answers.

Q.   How would you look on feeling a pulse which proved natural and regular?

A.   Very serious and I would pretend to be calculating.

Patient: 'I've been awfully troubled lately, Doctor, with my breathing.'
Doctor: 'Hum! I'll soon give you something to stop that.'

Q. A lady, slightly indisposed, asks whether you don't think her very ill – Your answer?

A. I should say that she would have been so if she hadn't sent for me in time.

'I get a sharp pain every time I do this, Doctor.'

Q.   Suppose a patient, in perfect health, demands what
     you think of his case?

A.   I should tell him, very mysteriously, that he ought to
     take care of himself.

'How is she today. Doctor?'

Appropriate Examination Paper:
with Answers.

Q. What should be the medical treatment of a common cold, which, in fact, requires only white-wine-whey and a footpan.

A. *Pulv: Antim:* grains five, to be taken at bed-time: and *Mistura Feb:* three table-spoonfuls every three hours, with *Emplast: Picis* to the region of the chest.

'This is really kind of you to call. Can I offer you anything—a basin of gruel, or a glass of cough mixture? Don't say no.'

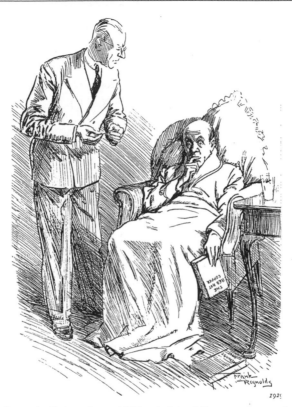

Doctor (to flu convalescent): 'Why, dash it all. Your temperature's gone up again. What have you been doing?'
Patient: 'Nothing. It's Edgar Wallace!'

Appropriate Examination Paper:
with Answers.

Q. An anxious mother, Sir, sends for you to see her darling child—What would you first do?

A. Begin by admiring it.

'I'm afraid, Ma'am, the little man has German Measles.'

Q. How long, in a given case, would you send in medicine?

A. As long a the patient believed himself ill.

Q. That belief being erroneous, what would you send, pray?

A. I think, *Tinct: Card: Comp:* with either *Aqua Menthæ Pip:* or *Mist: Camph.*

'And on your way here, Doctor, would you mind calling at the fishmonger's?'

Q. Be so good, Sir, as to translate the word 'Iter.'

A. Five shillings.

PERCIVAL LEIGH

Our Stout Cook: 'What's this?' 'Medical attendance two-an'-six!'
'Well, that's a good 'un! Why I attended on 'im! An' 'ad to wait
for two hours in that there surgery!'

17

Doctor: 'What did you operate on Jones for?'
Surgeon: 'A hundred pounds.'
Doctor: 'No, I mean what had he got?'
Surgeon: 'A hundred pounds.'

• COUGHING UP •

REFORM YOUR DOCTORS' BILLS
[1853]

How to pay honestly and fairly for medical advice may have been a problem to a few of our readers, most of whom, being entirely constitutional, have had few dealings with the doctor. A help towards the solution thereof has been furnished in an extract from a letter in the *Morning Herald,* the writer of which, speaking of Californian practice, says that 'for three "ahems!" and a "ha!" he paid in August last twenty-seven dollars.' Hence may be derived a scheme for the reformation of doctors' bills. To charge a shilling or eighteenpence for a draught consisting of an infusion of rose holding neutral salt in solution, value one penny, would be a monstrosity, did we not know that the practitioner's education, knowledge, and abilities are supposed to be dissolved along with the *Magnes. Sulph.* in the *Infus. Rosæ.* But this is merely a supposition. You can't dissolve medical science and skill, either in *Infus. Rosæ*, or *Mist. Camphoræ*, or *Aqua Pura*, or *Aqua Pump*. Why, then, should not medical practitioners follow out the Californian notion, and charge for their opinions, as expressed in their interjections? As, for instance—

	s.	d.
Humph!	2	6
Ha!	1	6
Oho!	3	0
Indeed!	4	6
Well, well!	5	0

The idea might be extended, so that the scale of fees should rise proportionably with the elongation of the professional utterances: as thus

	s.	d.
Put out your Tongue	6	8
Let me feel your Pulse	13	6

But here we forbear; considering that our recommend-ation to charge—addressed to doctors—must appear to patients rather like the exhortation, 'Up, guards, and at them.'

PERCIVAL LEIGH

Country Practitioner: 'I shan't be more than ten days at the furthest, Mr. Fawceps. You'll visit the patients regularly, and take care that none of them slip through your fingers—or get well—during my absence!'

THE MEDICAL
• STUDENT •

Son of the scalpel! from whatever class
You grind instruction just enough to pass
St George's, Guy's, North London, or King's
    College—
Thirsting alike for half-and-half and knowledge—
Thou who must know so well, (all jibes apart,)
The true internal structure of the heart—
This heart – which you 'a hollow muscle' call,
I offer thee – aorta, valves, and all.
Though to cheap hats and boots thy funds incline,
And light rough Chesterfields at one pound nine:
Though on the virtues of all plants thou'rt dumb
Save the *Nicotiana Tabacum*,
(*Pentandria Digynia!* – Lindley – mum!)

❊ ❊ ❊ ❊ ❊

Though thou eschewest the hospital's dull gloom.

Except to chat in the house-surgeon's room,
And practically practise, in addition,
The 'Physiology of Deglutition.'
Yet much I love thee, and devoutly swear
With lips that move controll'd by 'the fifth pair,'
That I will never know peace until our hands
Shall form a 'ganglion' with Hymen's bands.

Then haste, my love, and let me call thee mine
Precious and dear as sulphate of quinine,
Sparkling and bright as antimonial wine,
Sharp as the angles of a new trephine,
My reckless, noisy, fearnought VALENTINE!

ANON

1846   1886

'You're sure you feel all right—I can hear a sonata in F minor by Brahms.'

THE
• SPECIALIST •

THE EXPERT WHO COULD TELL
WITHOUT LOOKING
[1925]

It was Harley Street, and the Great Man himself was bending over me.

My own doctor had sent me there as an 'interesting case'. This, I shrewdly suspected without prejudice to his right to make me a small charge on his own account for having invested my apparently trifling ailment with such a gratifying atmosphere of distinction.

For what seemed like half-an-hour (it was really sixty seconds) the Great Man glared at me. I began to feel convinced that I had committed some heinous offence against the rules of healthy living and was going to be

'This is the one I wear if they ask for a second opinion.'

made to pay the penalty. I wondered how much funerals cost nowadays.

Suddenly he frightened me almost out of my skin by speaking.

'Your case is deeply interesting,' he said. 'Curiously enough I have only met two others like it during over thirty years' practice. Stranger still both these came to

'We must on no account permit anyone to give us a shock, Mr. Pembridge. The least shock of any sort would in our present state of health be sure to kill us immediately.'

'Sir Charles is attending a very important appendix, Madame.'

me within a day or two of each other, about twelve months ago. Most remarkable coincidence of all, perhaps, each left a widow and seven children. I think you said you have seven yourself, didn't you?'

He paused impressively. I coughed but didn't attempt to answer his question. Somehow I don't think he really meant me to.

'Now doubtless you imagine,' he continued, 'that I am going to carve you up or fill you to the brim with pills and potions. Completely mistaken, my dear Sir. Completely, I assure you.'

He paused again, washing his hands with invisible soap. His eyes shone, apparently in joyous anticipation of some devilry even more than dissection.

'Ninety per cent of digestive troubles,' he resumed, 'are now known to be due merely to bad teeth. Clear away the teeth and you clear away the indigestion.'

Once more he paused beamed expansively, and waggled a fat forefinger at me with elephantine waggishness.

'To cure your complaint,' he continued unctuously. 'I shall have to pass you on to the dental specialist next door; a little expensive perhaps, but easily the best man in Europe. You can never hope to enjoy normal health again until every tooth in your head has been extracted.'

It was at this point that I grasped my plates and reverently bared my totally toothless gums.

INFLUENZA VIRUS DISCOVERED AT A LONDON HOSPITAL

'The Influenza microbe' announces a medical journal, 'has made its appearance in many parts of the country and is slowly but surely making its way towards London.' With any other Government than ours a simple suggestion that the sign posts en route should be reversed would have been at once adopted.

11 February 1920

FASHIONABLE
• AILMENTS •

A FUTURE COMPLAINT
[1932]

Now that 'declines' have gone right out and inherited gout is still largely the perquisite of the aristocracy as subject-matter for angry and virile anecdote, human nature, ever casting about for ailments of which to complain, finds its stock running low.

Blood-pressure is *passé*; even colitis is *demodé*. Influenza has long been rejected on the ground that to mention that one 'has flu' is, as it were, to sneeze at too crowded an altar.

With amazing unanimity a number of my friends have selected their ailment for the coming season.

It is loss of memory. This is going to be all the rage soon. 'I can't remember a *thing*' is the slogan when you try to pin anybody down to anything. Therefore for those who would be in the swim I append a few suggestions culled from the antics of my own circle, hoping that with a minimum of thought and effort we may all soon become the complete Heedless Butterfly, and always bearing in what you deliberately retain of your mind that the cult of failing memory may be closely allied to the slightly less distinguished absence of mind. The point is that your doings should be capable of relation as proof of your mental condition.

You can start at any age over twenty-five. Apparently your failure to remember may take various forms, and you needn't confine yourself merely to omitting to telephone the butcher for sweetbreads. Nor need you forget only two dinner engagements and a bridge tea, but it is distinctly a point scored if you arrive at the parties a week too early or a day too late.

Also it is pretty to go into the post-office for a two-shilling book of stamps and to ask instead for an eighteen-penny postal order or a licence for a Pekinese.

For your domestically-minded friends the story of how on the cook's day out you put the joint in the oven and forgot all about it until the house was filled with blue mist and you cried, 'Oh, Henry, the house is on fire!' will always prove popular.

Nerve Specialist: 'You must give up your cocktails and night-clubs and you must stop smoking.'
Lady: 'But I don't do any of those things.'
Nerve Specialist: 'And I will give you a letter to my friend Sir Julius Bronson. He will prescribe for your loss of memory.'

The verbal clowning of book-titles and authors offers a wide and fruitful field, as: 'Have you read *A Brass Band in No-Man's-Land*, by—Oh, dear, my head!' or 'I always think *Martin Nicklewit* is Dickens' best book'; or 'I *do* so admire J.—no, B. D.—or is it E. L.?—what'shisname's last novel. You know—the one where an actor-manager—no, that was by the other man, Thingummy, who wrote

Family Doctor: 'And no port, mind; if you drink port wine you'll have another attack of gout, as sure as faith.'
Country Gentleman: 'Quite certain?''
Family Doctor: 'No doubt about it.'
Country Gentleman: 'The very thing. You stay and dine; we'll have some of that "Thirty-four," and —I'm summoned on a jury the day after tomorrow!'

Patient: 'Doctor, my memory has recently become shockingly bad.'
Doctor: 'Indeed? In these cases, sir, it is my invariable rule to ask for my fee in advance.'

that other book we all liked so. Anyway, it had a red cover.'

If your listeners are in a literary set your verbal slips can become wilder, which will not only emphasise your impaired cerebration but will probably establish you as a wit into the bargain. Modern book-titles being what they are, it will be your own fault if you fail. And, while on the subject of books, many and strange are the mental capers you can cut while at your circulating library. You can (1) Omit to take back the book you want to change, or return one that has been the property of your family

'Of course you're not a nuisance, Mr Fitzgerald, one gets tired of dealing with trivial complaints all the time.'

for thirty years; (2) Leave your book-list and 'token' at home and bring the washing-book instead; (3) Secure your new book and, leaving it on the counter, take home the one you have just returned. You then read the book once more in perfect good faith, and it makes the story better if you enjoyed it thoroughly and didn't find out it was the old book until the last chapter.

Having secured the attention of the table at dinner, begin a story, and suffer it to peter out, thanks to your inability to recollect the dénouement and the names of the persons of the narrative. This is especially effective when retailing scandal. Your faltering apology will be received with many polite noises of interest and commiseration and nobody will think you are tipsy. They will all know that your brain is not what it was, and that, in fine, you are In the Movement.

Extremes should of course be avoided; that is to say that 'to forget your own name next' is only allowable when adducing instances of the lengths to which in time, your feeble faculty may drive you. Actually it is not a plausible move. Nor, unless at bay for social success, should loss of identity be adopted, for this will get you no further than the newspapers and may lead to your having to spend a night at the police-station.

The best move of all is to give a dinner yourself and

leave the house at seven o'clock for a restaurant and the theatre. Or, if you you shy at so extreme a measure (though you need fear nothing, for arrogance and discourtesy are distinctly smart), you can descend to the drawing-room, betraying a charming surprise at finding it full of friends—and clad in complete skating-kit. Thus your guests will secure their dinner, no bad feelings will be harboured and you will become A Whimsical overnight.

Only remember one thing: Forget *something*—no matter what it is, and your May and June should be unusually brilliant.

RACHEL

'Bet you didn't get those on the Health Service.'

FASHIONS IN PHYSIC [1890]

[The President of the British Pharmaceutical Conference lately drew
attention to the prevalence of fashion in medicine.]

A fashion in physic, like fashions in frills:
The doctors at one time are mad upon pills;
And crystalline principles now have their day,
Where alkaloids once held an absolute sway.
The drugs of old times might be good, but it's true.
We discard them in favour of those that are new.

The salts and the senna have vanished, we fear,
As the poet has said, like the snows of last year;
And where is the mixture in boyhood we quaff'd.
That was known by the ominous name of Black
    Draught?
While Gregory's Powder has gone, we are told,
To the limbo of drugs that are worn out and old.

New fads and new fancies are reigning supreme,
And calomel one day will be but a dream;
While folks have asserted a chemist might toil
Through his shelves, and find out he had no castor oil;
While as to Infusions, they've long taken wings,

And they'd think you quite mad for prescribing such
    things.

The fashion to-day is a tincture so strong,
That, if dosing yourself you are sure to go wrong.
What men learnt in the past they say brings them no
    pelf.
And the well-tried old remedies rest on the shelf.
But the patient may haply exclaim, 'Don't be rash.
Lest your new-fangled physic should settle my hash.'
MR CLARKE

So many doctors have been
telling us the dangers of kiss-
ing that there is some talk of
putting an antiseptic lipstick
on the market.

2 May 1928

NON PLACEBO

The Minister of Health has banned from prescription under the National Health scheme more than six hundred drugs 'of little or no medicinal value.' This is a facer for the doctors, who must still find something to give patients with little or nothing the matter with them.

21 October 1953

Apprentice: 'If you please, sir, shall I fill up Mrs. Twaddle's draught with water?'

Practitioner: 'Dear, Dear me, Mr Bumps, how often must I mention the subject? We never use water— "Aqua destillata," if you please!'

DOCTORS
& THEIR
• PRESCRIPTIONS •

THE MYSTERY OF MEDICINE
[1845]

We perceive that Mr. Muntz has given notice of a motion requiring all medical practitioners to write their prescriptions in English, and to put plain English on their gallipots. If this proposal is adopted, the dignity of Medicine is gone, for on the principle of *omne ignotum pro magnifico*, people fancy that a prescription must do them a wonderful deal of good if they cannot understand the meaning of it. Who will have any faith in medicine when he knows the ingredients?

There is something mysterious in *Duæ pilulæ jactæ cum pane*, but when we come to know that it means nothing more than 'two bread pills,' the senses revolt against the idea of deriving any benefit from taking them. Besides, when a medical man is in a hurry, and does not know exactly what to prescribe, he can always with safety scribble down *Aq.—Cochl.—pan.—Sen.—Mag.—Cort.*, and the apothecary, if he has any tact, will send in something harmless, with directions at his own discretion about the mode and period of taking it.

But if all prescriptions are to be in English, what on earth is a medical man to do when he wants to prescribe nothing at all, but a dose quite at the discretion of the chemist. We knew a facetious general practitioner who used to jot down *quod—plac—mi—form—car*, which looked very well in abbreviated Latin, but which was in short – or rather in full – *quoduncque places, mi formosa care* – (whatever you please, my pretty dear;) a prescription the chemist always understood to mean water with a dash of senna in it, to be taken at bedtime. We entreat Mr. Muntz to pause before he strips medicine of that mystery which gives it half its importance in the eyes of the multitude. As to anglicising the gallipots we defy the best linguist on earth to translate into English those mystic syllables which are painted at random with a view to variety, and without the remotest attempt at meaning.

OUR OVERWORKED
DOCTORS

A London doctor types his prescriptions. He is said to be sensitive about his legible handwriting.

WHAT PARSONS PRESCRIBE
[1853]

Many surgeons, doubtless, remarked an absurd letter from a clergyman which appeared the other day in *The Times*, recommending charcoal – in combination with brandy and opium – as a cure for cholera. One of them, dating his letter from Bloomsbury Square, has fortunately written an answer to that communication, pointing out that the quantity of the last-named drug prescribed by the parson would amount to 10 or 12 grains every half-hour; and of course destroy the patient. This clergyman, no doubt, is a well-meaning person, but he should confine himself to pointing the way to Heaven, recollecting that the opposite place is paved with good intentions. Possibly he overstated the quantity of opium, by what may be called a clerical error; a proper dose of it is well known to be beneficial in the complaint in question: brandy is also found useful: and to these two ingredients of the mixture we should be disposed to ascribe any favourable result of its administration. The third is probably inert; otherwise it would be a convenient medicine, as anybody, in case of need, might munch cinders.

Clergymen, in their anxiety to do good, are too often

Doctor: 'Um! Most insolent! ' (to his wife) 'Listen to this my dear. "Sir, —I enclose a P.O. Order for thirteen shillings and sixpence, hoping it will do you as little good as your very small bottles of Physic did me."'

accustomed to add the treatment of bodies to the cure of souls. In order to minister to patients as well as penitents, they ought to possess the gift of healing, and that having ceased to be supernaturally imparted, they had better acquire it in the ordinary manner, by attending the hospitals.

PERCIVAL LEIGH

'My dear—he simply twisted my subconscious
round his little finger.'

ON DIET AND
• LIFESTYLE •

THIS HEALTH HABIT
[1932]

Dear 'Medical Correspondent' I know you mean well but I wish you wouldn't. There is something hypnotic about your newspaper contributions which compels me to listen to Doris when she reads them out, or even, in my weaker moments to read them myself.

Doris I may mention has her one invariable method of referring to any newspaper-writer however distinguished 'It says here…' she begins and if 'it' says anything about calorific values or deep breathing or the risks of something or other I know by instinct that you are 'it.' You have got a grip on our household, and that's a fact. If my grandchildren are not born with a pretty shattering 'health-complex' it will be no fault of yours.

Now I have no objection to your telling me how to

PRECAUTIONARY MEASURES

Local Practitioner (as he goes through his day-book and ledger): 'Old Smith hasn't called me in lately about his indigestion. ... You'd better ask him to dinner.'

guard against seasonable ailments. That's sound stuff, and if only I could remember and had time to follow your advice I am sure I should be much less of a wart in the eyes of the medical profession. I don't even mind your asking me those personal questions such as 'Do You Sleep Sensibly?' 'Can You See Straight?' 'Are You Your Stomach's Enemy?' and other posers which a less intimate writer would hesitate to put to the most constant of readers.

NOT TO BE TAKEN LITERALLY

Doctor: 'Well, we must try that diet, Mrs. Podger, and if it doesn't
answer, the—er—patient must fall back on eggs!'

WISE IN HIS GENERATION

Fashionable Patient: 'Cod-liver oil!!! My dear doctor. I couldn't take such horrible stuff as that!'
Fashionable Doctor: 'Well—well—What do you say to—a—cream and curaçao?'

No what I resent is your increasing habit of pouncing upon certain of our sports and pastimes and gutting them, so to speak, of pretty well everything except their confounded 'health' elements.

Through men like you thousands of us have been induced to give up walking for pleasure and take to hiking for health. We have no time now on our peregrinations to commune with Nature or dream noble dreams; we are

52

far too heavily engaged in wondering whether we are dressed according to your hygienic prescription, whether we are swinging from the waist (or whatever it is you say we ought to swing from), whether our diaphragm is functioning according to the rules, what our skin is absorbing and how other important bits of us are getting on. Some of us dare not even pause to sniff the scents of earth and hedgerow because we have forgotten what you said regarding The Right Way to Sniff. Even the sight of our picturesque goal arouses no elation; we are too worried as to whether we shall be able to get enough of the right kind of vitamins at the local inn.

Thanks to you, many who used to enjoy a game of lawn tennis now take scientific exercise about the court for the sake of doing themselves good. Myriads immerse themselves in water, not from the old fashioned motive of sheer physical gratification, but as a grim preparation for the hygienic rigours of sun-bathing. There have even been cases of people *singing* in their baths for health.

If you ask me (which you never do), this health complex of yours is causing you to break out in far too many spots. I believe you would have our cricketers take the field as though they were doing a health-cure, their every movement and stance conforming to the printed instruc-

A LUCID INTERVAL

Doctor: 'How is the patient this morning?'

Nurse: 'Well—He has been wandering a good deal in his mind. Early this morning I heard him say, "What an old woman that doctor is!"—and I think that was about the last really *rational* remark he made.'

tions and diagrams (Side Fielding, for Use of) issued by an M.C.C. Medical Advisory Board. You would handicap golfers according to the amount of benefit the game conferred upon a player's bi-uvular glands, if any. You would love to insist upon billiards players breathing through the ears; you would like to show village boys how to leap-frog so as to improve the abdominal muscles; and if you had your way you would put a set of Hints on Physical Deportment inside every box of tiddly-winks.

Further words fail me, and anyhow the moment has come when I am scheduled to put on my little cellular pants and do a spot of hygienic gardening.

Yours under protest,   D. C.

A Brighton man who was given up by doctors forty years ago lived to the age of one hundred and three. This shows the kind of thing that medical men have to put up with.

MY DOCTOR

My doctor's a capital fellow;
    He may not possess a degree,
But his counsel's as shrewd as it's mellow
    And there's never a hint of a fee.

Each day he attends to my diet,
    For he's keenly aware of the food
That will cause me internal disquiet
    And the kind that will do me most good.

He can gauge more or less to a minute
    The amount of repose I require,
The rules I must follow to win it
    And the time when I ought to retire.

To a pipeful he's able to ration
    The smokes I can safely consume,
And is prompt to encourage my passion
    For inviting fresh air to a room.

For my health I am hourly his debtor;
    Though for ills he can offer no cure
He believes that prevention is better,
    More simple, attractive and sure.

In his forties a man must grow wiser
If he wouldn't be laid on the shelf;
And this medical friend and adviser,
Between you and me, is myself.

A.K.

'Hulloah, my boy, you *have* been putting on weight!'
'Can't help it. Doctor's orders. Said I was only to drink at meals.
Got to eat such a dooce of a lot of meals, don't you know.'

THE DOCTOR
AS
• PATIENT •

HEAL THYSELF

[1953]

The public always appear surprised that doctors should fall ill, as though hearing that a policeman's house had been burgled or the fire station had gone up in flames. Doctors go sick fairly often, though they suffer differently from anyone else: they have only one disease, which presents both a *mitis* and a *gravis* form.

The *mitis* phase is characterized clinically by the usual symptoms of malaise, headache, shivering, loss of appetite, coughing, and insomnia. It usually lasts several days, while the doctor does his surgery sitting in an overcoat and wonders why he's becoming so bad-tempered. He shakes off his symptoms like a wet dog and makes a diagnosis of draughts, late nights, or over-work.

When he wakes up one morning with black shapes in

'You need a holiday.'
'But, Doctor, I've just had one.'
'Then I do.'

front of his eyes he sneaks down to the surgery in his dressing-gown and stealthily takes his temperature. A hundred and four! This immediately ushers in the *gravis* stage of the illness. He snatches a textbook from the shelf and nervously flicks over the pages. The first disease he spots is typhoid fever. *Prostration … headache … cough … backache …* he reads, running his finger quickly along the symptomatology. He realizes nervously he has

'Hullo—and how's the doctor this morning?'

every one of these afflictions, locks the door, and tries to feel his own spleen.

Admitting he is a desperately ill man he staggers to bed, bringing with him every medical and surgical textbook he can lay hands on. Once comfortable on the pillows he can see the problems of diagnosis more clearly. There are several more alarming diseases than typhoid to attract him, and after a while he becomes certain he is in the grip of either cholera, smallpox, or plague. He takes his pulse, inspects his tongue in his wife's hand-mirror, and carries out a careful search of his entire body-surface for spots. Finally he settles for malignant endocarditis, a diagnosis that in his finals would have had him thrown out of the examination room.

He next faces the problem of treatment. Doctors' houses are well supplied with drugs by the manufacturing chemists, who supplement their advertisements in the morning mail with transparently-

Anxious Patient: 'When I wake in the morning I feel just terrible.'
Festive Physician: 'Not worse than I do. I'll wager.'

wrapped packets of samples. These are always stuffed into the bathroom cabinet where old tooth-paste tubes, rusty razor blades, and worn fragments of soap accumulate. Dragging himself out of bed, he finds a bottle of bright green pills and wonders what they are. He swallows a few and rummages about until he comes across some aspirins. Several more coloured packets then attract him, and he starts mixing himself a therapeutic *hors d'oeuvre*.

'...and now would you like a second opinion?'

Doctors require different doses from the general public. The patient who goes away with a prescription marked sternly 'one teaspoonful in an egg-cupful of water every four hours' is frightened enough to assemble spoon, egg-cup, and kitchen clock and takes the dose as precisely as starting a race. But in the profession pills are generally taken in doses of 'One Handful Now and Then' (or if they are particularly small ones, 'About a Dozen'), medicine administered as 'A Large Swig Pretty Frequently', and ointments and embrocations assumedly labelled 'Rub on Vigorously Until Alarmed by the Condition of the Skin'.

Doctors recover in a different way from ordinary people. A layman is told to stay in bed for an extra week and take a fortnight at the seaside; but a doctor, after taking his temperature every half-hour for a day or so, suddenly discovers he is completely cured. He at once gets up and puts on his clothes, and either goes downstairs and takes the evening surgery or makes for the garden to catch up with his digging.

As most doctors will admit, they can't afford to be ill: they're not registered as patients under the National Health Service.

RICHARD GORDON

THE DOCTOR